Rabbit's Journey

Grace Gemini

Blue Dragon Press
Maryland

Published by Blue Dragon Press
http://BlueDragonPress.com

ISBN 978-1-62220-021-4, POD

To Jesse Elia

who taught me
that wisdom often comes
from unexpected places

PREFACE

Rabbit *can be viewed as an allegory for adults on a personal journey, or as a children's story. See the Author's Note at the end for my lessons from* *Rabbit*.

There is an exercise designed to help an individual find their power animal. You enter a meditative state and ask for your power animal to appear. Eventually you will visualize an animal approaching you. Each Power Animal has different gifts and abilities, and by accompanying us through our lives; whether for a long time or for just a short while, the animal spirits draw our attention to areas in our lives which could benefit from their particular skills.

I got all excited about this exercise. I knew the animals I'd been drawn to ever since I was a little girl: the deer, the owl, the otter, and, most recently, the bear. I thought I had a pretty good idea of what was going to show. *Oh, I just* ***know*** *it will be Bear—I need Bear's strength!* and *But what if it's Owl? I could use Owl's stealth. Or Deer's swiftness? Or maybe...?*

So there I was, visualizing myself in a field at the edge of a forest, waiting for some grand and powerful spirit to come out of the woods towards me.

Well, something did show up, and much to my surprise, it was not any of the animals I had counted on ... instead, out of the shadows came ... a rabbit.

A RABBIT?!?! I said to myself, *What can a rabbit do?* I wasn't sure how to take this. It certainly wasn't one of the traditional creatures you'd expect, but still this animal spirit must have something to tell me, so I decided to think on it a little more. Eventually, I felt a story coming on ... .

Rabbit's Journey
Grace Gemini

Rabbit was nervous.

Her nose and whiskers twitched as she looked up at the circle of creatures gathered around her. From her place in the crowd, she could see the tiny red eyes of the field mice; unblinking and wary.

The deer stamped their dainty hooves and dug long grooves in the soft ground while nearby wolves struggled to keep their curious pups from running into the middle of the circle to pounce upon whatever imaginary foes were lurking there.

Many others had come down from the trees or crept up from their burrows to attend the meeting. Partridges, wrens and owls set up their own choruses and sang their songs loudly. It looked as though every creature ever known was packed into the clearing but even with the tumult, something tickled at the back of Rabbit's mind--something was missing.

All around Rabbit, eyes shifted, noses wrinkled, tails swept, beaks clicked, ears perked; and still they waited for Bear to arrive. Bears lived by their own time, it was true; everyone knew that, so there was nothing left to do but wait.

The twittering, whistling, growling gathering became louder and louder; and just when it seemed as though Rabbit could bear it no longer, all fell silent.

Bear lumbered up the path and took his spot on the Bigrock at one end of the clearing. Bear was so big that even Bigrock, the ancient meeting point for all the forest animals, seemed like little more than a river pebble next to him. It was said that Bear was almost as old as the stone, and it certainly looked possible, given the silver hairs that covered his snout and shoulders. He was very wise; he walked with spirits and the shades of things only seen by eyes that were opened. Bear commanded the respect of every creature who called the forest its home.

Bear tossed his great, shaggy head once and scanned the crowd with his eyes. His measuring gaze fell upon each creature in turn, and when he got to Rabbit, she felt as though it lingered on her face for just a second longer than any one else's. Rabbit shivered.

Then Bear spoke, and his voice was like the rumble of the rain-swollen river in Springtime. "I have called you here," he began, "because I need your help. Blue Jay is missing."

Blue Jay! Rabbit gasped. Now she knew what had been missing! She scanned the crowd once more--sure enough; no Blue Jay.

"What happened to him?" yelled a young fox.

"We don't know," replied Bear, "but we did find this." Bear raised his massive arm. Clenched in his paw was a feather; a blue feather.

Rabbit remembered Blue Jay. She remembered all the animals that lived in the woods. The likenesses of those animals were carved upon the great Ancestor Pole which stood in the middle of the forest. There were wolves, and coyotes, mountain lions and bobcats, eagles and falcons.

There were many more that Rabbit had never seen. Like those who had no arms or legs, and lived, she was told, in something like a lake only much, much bigger. And, of course, there were blue jays. Every animal spirit was represented. The blue jays had always been kind to Rabbit. Their calls were among some of the loudest in the forest; Rabbit could always count on them to raise a warning when a predator was near.

Bear cleared his throat, which sounded more like a roar. "I'm convinced that Blue Jay did not leave the forest on his own. I need volunteers to go look for him."

Wolf stepped forward, as everyone knew he would. Wolf was very brave. "I will help to look for Blue Jay," he said. There were nods all around the circle. Wolf was a good choice.

Owl also entered the circle. Owl was a great hunter, and it might be useful to be able to search from the air. Owl swiveled her head back and forth to take in the approving looks of her fellow creatures.

No other animal dared make a move. Voles and weasels gathered their young around them and shook their furry heads. The badgers stared down at their paws in silence.

"Is there no one else?" growled Bear.

Rabbit gulped and stepped forward on her big, flat feet. "I'll go," she said.

The crowd was stunned. Then they began to laugh. "A rabbit?!" one cried. "Oh of course, now why didn't I think of that before? A rabbit is a most fearsome and dangerous creature!" The animals dissolved in peals of laughter. Rabbit only stood there, looking straight ahead, right into Bear's brown eyes. What help could she give to these two hunters? Still, Blue Jay was her friend.

"I will go," she said once more; hoping she sounded braver than she felt.

"Then it is settled," said Bear. "You three will leave immediately."

"Just don't slow us down Rabbit," growled Wolf.

Wolf and Owl took off and headed deeper into the forest. It was all Rabbit could do to keep up with them.

After running full speed for what seemed like hours, they saw the trees begin to thin. Wolf stopped short at the edge of a large meadow and Rabbit skidded to a halt beside him. The grass was tall and dry and there was a little hill which blocked their view of the other end of the field. The wind was blowing towards them, bearing a strange sort of haze. Owl circled overhead. Wolf sniffed the air suspiciously.

"I smell something," he growled. Rabbit just stared at the ground beneath her paws and panted miserably.

Owl landed silently in front of them. "Smoke," she said. "There's a brush fire on the other side of the hill, at the far end of the meadow. It goes in a straight line for as far as I can see. There isn't a way around it for miles, and it's moving this way."

"So we can't get around it before it reaches us," said Wolf. "Over it?" he asked, looking at Owl.

"I already tried," she said. "The smoke rises too high, I lost all sense of direction up there. We could turn back, or try another path," she continued. "We don't really know if Blue Jay came this way or not anyway."

"Yes we do," said Rabbit, who had been quiet up until then. She was still staring at the ground. Beneath her paws was another blue feather.

Rabbit eyed the dry grass in dismay. The fire-line was moving toward them fast.

"Not over it," she said. "And around it would take too long, so that leaves ... I know! Follow me!" she cried. Rabbit ran as fast as she could ... *toward* the fire!

Wolf and Owl exchanged confused looks, and then took off after Rabbit.

They ran as far as the rise of the hill and then stopped. Then Rabbit began to dig--and dig she did--faster than she had ever dug before!

"*Under* it!" she cried. "I can burrow under it! You two enter the burrow behind me!"

Rabbit's paws pushed the earth behind her as she continued down into the soil. Soon there was enough room for Wolf, then Owl; and they both crammed into the tunnel as far as they could go. The trio was well underground when the line of fire on the surface moved over them, crackling loudly. A few moments more and they were climbing out a hole on the other side of it. Rabbit cleaned the dirt off her face delicately with her paws. Wolf shook himself vigorously, flinging dust and bits of earth in all directions.

Owl just blinked, and looked backwards at the charred grass on the hillside. "That's an experience I don't care to repeat," she said. She turned and looked forward, "It looks like it gets pretty rocky from here." The ground rose quickly in front of them, broken in spots by moss-covered boulders and thorny bushes. "You two had best watch your footing."

Wolf looked forward, squinting his eyes. "We're close to the mountains," he said. Wolf gave a sidelong glance in Rabbit's direction. "You can ride on my back if you like … just so you won't be so slow. We're in a hurry you know."

Rabbit nodded—best not to beleaguer the point, she thought. She climbed on Wolf's back and the three continued on towards the mountains.

Mountain travel did not come easily to Rabbit. The height made her dizzy and she disliked the alarming manner in which Wolf's back swayed from side to side (*how could anything this furry be this bony*?) as he picked his way through the rocks. For animals used to the cool, damp shadows and mossy floor of the forests; this rising, dry, rocky world was completely alien. No one said a word. They just set their jaws determinedly forward and continued on their grim journey to … well, nobody actually knew to where, but they were sure it was this way.

It was Owl, with her sharp eyes, who spotted the next blue feather, lying at the mouth of a wide crack in the rocks. Wolf got down on his belly and peered over the edge.

"It goes down pretty far, but I can't see anything else," he said. His weight dislodged pebbles from around the rim, sending bits skittering into the darkness.

"There's a floor down there," said Rabbit. Her big ears were strained forward. "I heard the little rocks hit bottom."

"I didn't hear a thing," said Owl. "Must be those big ears of yours."

Rabbit nodded. She thought she heard something else ... the sound of rushing water.

"Well, one thing's for certain," growled Wolf, "We won't be able to see anything if we go down there. We should look around some more; this tunnel must come up somewhere. Maybe there's a way to bypass it."

Getting up, Wolf raised his hind legs first, which was a mistake as he had forgotten that Rabbit was on his back. Her weight on his shoulders over-balanced him and he tumbled head-first into the hole with Rabbit still clinging to his fur. They hit bottom with a muted *thump*!

Wolf groaned. He could see the sunlight shining through the hole on the surface. It seemed impossibly far away, and Owl was just a speck peeking down. Dust floated through the air, but outside the shaft of sunlight, all was darkness.

Owl sighed and shook her head. In a moment, she was down beside the other two. "Now what?" she said. "I can't lift either of you."

"Wait a moment," Rabbit turned her head to one side. "I hear water. Doesn't water always flow downhill?"

"I believe it does, but what of it?" said Wolf, who was more than a little annoyed with their predicament.

"I understand," Owl explained. "We won't be able to see, but Rabbit can *hear* the water. If *she* follows the sound, and *we* follow *her*, we can follow the river out."

Wolf considered, "That will only work if there's a path all the way through here."

"There has to be," said Rabbit. "If there had been a fire for light you'd have smelled it by now, right?" Wolf nodded. "Well, Blue Jay couldn't fly in the dark and so he had to have been walking." Rabbit didn't finish aloud, but she thought to herself, *I hope … .*

Wolf rolled his eyes, "Alright, you win. We don't have a better choice."

Rabbit nodded and closed her eyes. Her ears twitched. In a little while, she chose a direction, "This way."

Wolf caught her tail gently between his teeth and Owl took hold of his. Together they ventured out of the circle of light, and into the blackness beyond.

It was slow going. All three animals were completely blind. Luckily, Rabbit was right, and there was a ledge that ran along the river, but it was narrow and very slippery. Even with Rabbit's hearing, it was difficult to keep to the path. The tunnel split and re-split. Sound bounced off the rock walls, and off itself to create maddening echoes that threatened to turn Rabbit completely around. Often the underground river passed beneath some unseen formation to reappear on the other side. One wrong step would send Rabbit over the edge and into the water, dragging her companions with her. *Oh I hope this was the right thing to do*, thought Rabbit to herself. She wasn't so afraid for her own sake, but she was acutely afraid for the sake of her new friends. *Friends? Well, why not?*

Instead of growing fainter, the sound of the water was getting much, much louder. Even Wolf and Owl could hear it now.

"I smell fresh air up ahead," said Wolf.

"I can see some light in front of us," replied Owl.

The opening of the tunnel came into view around a curve in the wall. The river was wider here, and it flowed out the hole in the rocks where it just ... disappeared into the light beyond. The narrow ledge ended abruptly at the mouth of the tunnel. Wolf, Owl and Rabbit followed the flow of water with their eyes and were shocked. It traveled to the edge of a huge cliff, and then continued *straight down*! The source of the roar was quite apparent now. The path had ended and there was nothing more in front of them except a massive waterfall, with a drop that seemed to go on forever.

The three surveyed the landscape below. The river ran swiftly and strongly in the channel it had cut between mountains of stone. The water foamed in white eddies around the slimy, gray-green boulders that broke the surface. Slippery rocks, sheer walls, white water, fast currents.

"It seems that down is not an option," said Wolf.

"There are no trees," said Owl. "I don't like this place."

It was true; there were no trees, only short, scrubby things sprouting from cracks in the rocks. They looked as though growing leaves was something they just didn't have the inspiration to do.

There were large, thorny clumps of them to the sides of the cave entrance, and a few clinging to the canyon walls but nothing else. Even the sky seemed gray.

The sun passed behind a cloud and Rabbit shivered in the resulting shadows ... but wait, that was no cloud! Rabbit hissed a warning and the three retreated back into the blackness of the cave. Wolf pressed the others against the walls making a shield with his body.

What they saw made their eyes go wide with fright. A huge dragon had flown across the canyon and landed on the mountain somewhere above them. Its scaly bulk had cast a shadow that stretched from one wall almost to the other. They could hear the dry, scraping sound as it hauled itself across the rocks. Pebbles and dust rained down the mountainside for a time; then it was quiet again except for the incessant roar of the waterfall. The dragon hadn't seen them, but how long could they go un-noticed?

"A dragon," said Rabbit. "I thought those things were just stories."

"I wish they were," Owl sounded wistful.

"You've seen one before?" asked Wolf.

"No," Owl replied. "But my grand-sire did. They usually don't stray far from their homes, but he saw one. He said it was the scariest thing he had ever seen—said he hid in the hollow trunk of a tree for two days until it stopped doing whatever it was doing

and flew off again. I've always wanted to see one. I'll bet it has a nest up above us somewhere."

Rabbit nodded, and whispered, "Do you think … that thing has Blue Jay?"

"I hope not," said Wolf. He turned to Owl. "We'll wait until the sun goes down; it has to sleep some time. You have the best eyes; maybe if you hover in front of the cave you can spot a path along the wall. Then we'll climb up to the nest and see."

Rabbit crept silently from the mouth of the cave and nibbled through the stems of a few bushes. These, she carefully dragged back inside to provide some meager protection to hide them. Owl and Wolf nodded in approval and all three settled down behind the dry wall of twigs to wait for dark.

Night did not fall gently in this place. There were no colored clouds and no soothing, cooling breezes. Instead it felt as though the sun had turned its back on them. There was no gradual fading from light to dark; all was blackness as soon as the sun sank behind the ridge. The temperature dropped dramatically and the three companions shivered, damp and miserable at the mouth of the cave.

Owl had spotted a rough trail leading up the side of the mountain, but owls were gliders. They preferred to drop upon their prey from above. Owl found it difficult to manage the currents of the wind; beyond a certain point she could soar no higher.

Indeed, the wind was no friend to any of them. It gathered up dust and flung it into their faces with angry hands no matter what direction they turned. Soon, Wolf's brown and tan, Owl's black and white and Rabbit's brown were all the same shade of stone gray.

It was Rabbit who heard it first—the snatches and shreds of conversation whipped about by the wind. The air had a foul odor; even without Wolf's powerful nose, she could smell it. It was like the inside of birds' eggs when they had fallen from the nest and no chick was growing inside. Wolf's eyes watered, he was breathing through his mouth and he climbed with his head down, as if willing himself to move forward against the stench. Now the three were glad of their drab coloring. They were almost impossible to see against the rocks, but they could see what lay in front of them in savage, disturbing detail.

To Rabbit, the structure resembled an upside-down beaver's lodge, only much bigger and shallower. It was woven together with branches, brambles, flat stones, whole saplings, and the bones of things she couldn't identify. Rabbit shuddered, for in the center of the massive tangle was Blue Jay. He was wrapped so tightly in vines that he couldn't move at all. His head and feet were the only things visible.

For a moment, in her relief to have found him, Rabbit saw nothing else but Blue Jay. She almost called out to him, but Owl's dusty wings surrounded her and bade her be silent.

Wolf inclined his head slightly to the side and Rabbit followed the line of sight further up onto a steep promontory of granite. There, on the top of the rocks, leathery wings spread and head held back on top of a long segmented neck was the most fearsome creature she had ever seen. *A dragon!*

Wolf growled deep within his throat, his hunter's instincts surging to the forefront of his mind. They blocked out everything else with an urgent call to action. Owl, too, was caught up in the thrill of the hunter's mind. Never noisy to begin with, Owl now seemed to absorb the sound all around her, leaving a silent, black space from which her yellow eyes gleamed.

Only Rabbit was unsure. She had no experience as a hunter—carrots and cabbages didn't tend to flee when she approached. But she certainly knew the look, the stance, even the scent of a creature poised to attack.

Something was wrong—*very* wrong. *Think quick*, she told herself. *Did dragons eat birds?* She didn't know; but if he wasn't to be eaten, why was Blue Jay tied up? Perhaps the dragon was using Blue Jay to lure another animal to the nest? But she had seen the dragon in flight. It certainly didn't look as though it would have any trouble at all catching its own prey. No, no—it wasn't any of those things. Then why keep … suddenly it hit her! It hit her just as Wolf and Owl attacked.

"NO!" Rabbit screamed. "You don't understand!"

Wolf and Owl spared no time for stealth. They rushed in, each aimed at a different part of the dragon's body—Owl streaking toward the emerald eyes as Wolf leapt for the throat. To their credit, they did manage to take the dragon by surprise. Unfortunately, she didn't stay that way for long.

At the last second, she ducked her long, reptilian head so that Owl was forced to check herself in flight or impact on the sharp horns crowning the dragon's skull. The movement also served to place the dragon's formidable teeth in the path of Wolf's lunge. The dragon squinted slightly as she took in the sight of her two opponents.

Rabbit made for the nest. She was no fighter, but she could help Blue Jay. As she cleared the low wall of woven sticks, Blue Jay turned his head to her. "Rabbit!" he whispered, "Whatever are you doing here?"

"Rescuing you," she said simply. "But there's another problem." Rabbit looked over the vines that covered Blue Jay's body. She saw what she had been looking for. Up close the vines weren't as thick as she had feared, and they were wrapped around long, straight sticks so as to hold the sticks close to Blue Jay's body.

Rabbit nudged against his wing gently. Blue Jay closed his eyes tightly and groaned. The wing was broken.

"They're both broken," he said. "And a foot. There was some kind of storm ... I don't know what it was. I only know that the wind caught me and hurled me against the rocks in that valley before the cave. I remember crying out for help and waking up here."

"These aren't meant to hurt you," said Rabbit, running a practiced paw over the sticks. "They're splints. That creature must have carried you here and set both your wings and your leg. Wolf! Owl! We've got to stop them! They don't know! Do you think you could stand if I remove some of these vines?"

"Yes ... I think so," said Blue Jay.

Rabbit sheared quickly through the heaviest of them with her sharp teeth and pushed Blue Jay up into a sitting position.

On the rocky outcropping things were getting much worse. Owl dove for the dragon's head and was met by a cloud of smoke and reeking, sulfurous gas. She choked and fought for air; and had to swoop lower to clear her eyes. Flying blind, Owl hit the side of a tall formation of stones and fell to the ground, stunned.

Wolf saw Owl fall and continued his attack with renewed vigor. He faked for the dragon's throat once again; but this time when she ducked her head, Wolf veered suddenly to the right, jumped from the top of one clawed hand to her shoulder and sunk his long, canine fangs into the soft flesh behind her ear.

The dragon roared in fury and pain. She snapped her head from side to side but couldn't dislodge Wolf, whose teeth sank deeper and deeper. Wolf was covered in blood and hanging by his muzzle, but still he held on. The dragon raised her claws. She was going to remove this creature no matter what it took.

High in the air, the dragon's talons gleamed white and were deathly sharp. The claw reached the zenith of its arc and paused for a second. Wolf held his breath and waited for the impact that would surely kill him.

"WAIT!!" came a voice from the base of the rocks, "Wait, Wolf! Blue Jay is OK! This dragon helped him!"

"It's true!" called Blue Jay. He was braced against the wall of the nest, but he was definitely alive.

The dragon looked at the little bundle of fur quizzically. "For a long time I was alone, and now it seems I have four of you. Do you forest creatures never shy away from situations that could get you killed?"

She let forth a rumbling, hiccupping sound and for a second Rabbit thought the dragon was going to renew her attack. But instead the rumbling became more rhythmic and Rabbit realized that the dragon was laughing!

Wolf, with his teeth still lodged firmly in dragon-flesh looked first at Rabbit, then at Blue Jay and groaned.

"And now, my fine warrior," said the dragon, "if you would be so kind ... ?"

Wolf released his grip and tumbled to the ground. If there was ever a time when it was possible for a Wolf to look sheepish, this was the time.

Over by the rocks, Owl stirred. She swiveled her feathery head around and spotted Wolf, lying in a bloody heap at the dragon's feet. "Wolf!" she cried, "Is he ... ?"

"No, I am very much alive," he said gruffly. He rolled onto his side facing the rocks and would say no more.

It took some doing, but eventually Wolf let himself be led away from the rocks to a small stream where he could wash the blood from his fur.

The dragon looked down at Rabbit; Rabbit's entire family could have fit inside one claw. "I found your friend broken on the ground. I flew him here and set his wings. I had no idea it would cause me such distress." She did not say this unkindly, but Rabbit still cringed.

"I'm sorry, so very sorry," said Rabbit. "Bear sent us here to find Blue Jay."

The dragon's eyes opened slightly wider, "Bear sent you?"

"Yes."

The dragon nodded. Rabbit surmised that the alarmingly toothy grimace on her long face was the dragon equivalent of a smile. It was not comforting.

"Well then, for Bear's sake, I will return you to the edge of your wood. But I cannot go any farther. There are many who do not see the truth as you see it, little one."

At the edge of the forest, the five creatures made their good-byes. Owl, Wolf, Rabbit and Blue Jay, who was strapped to Wolf's back, watched the dragon's shape grow smaller until it disappeared completely over the mountain.

"Not a bad sort, if you can stand the smell," said Wolf.

Bear was waiting for them at Bigrock when they returned. His wise brown eyes settled on Rabbit, and he nodded. "You did well," he rumbled. "And my thanks to you all for returning our friend Blue Jay safely home."

To Rabbit, he said, "I can see that I made the right choice in you."

"But I was the one who said I would go … ," she replied.

"As I thought you might. More important than a hunter's strength, or a warrior's skill—more important than Owl's eyes, Wolf's nose or even your big ears—is that you see what is. When the others attacked blindly you used your intuition. You always started from 'what is'—the present moment. The others would surely have eliminated the foe—but it was *you* who eliminated the *fear*." Bear leaned close to Rabbit, his voice sounding like a rumble of distant thunder, "You see, there will *always* be dragons, but we don't have to worry about this one any more." Bear winked and continued.

"Blue Jay has many days of healing ahead of him, but thanks to you he is alive to do it."

"No," said Rabbit. "Blue Jay is alive thanks to the dragon. All I did was see the truth."

THE END

AUTHOR'S NOTES

I'm fond of saying that Rabbit wrote this story herself. Being that she's basically a shy creature, she wasn't comfortable with a showy and forceful presentation. Apparently, Rabbit teaches that sometimes subtlety is the answer.

A Rabbit's instinct when danger threatens is to focus and be still. As I thought about what Rabbit was trying to teach me, I realized how much of my life at that time could benefit from a little stillness and focus--the opportunity to hear that 'inner voice' which has the answer to everything. When Rabbit listened for the direction of the underground river, I imagined myself in the blackness with no other senses interfering, and I listened for that direction, that guidance.

The more I thought about it, the more I realized that the story of Rabbit was a good illustration of the Huna Principle called *Mana*—translated as 'all power comes from within.' (This is not—or perhaps it is—to be confused with the *Mana* referred to when we discuss the energy of manifestation.)

I view Rabbit's greatest asset as her ability to listen to her inner wisdom (perhaps that's why her ears were so big). That more than makes up for her lack of Wolf's ferocious strength or Owl's hunter's instinct. Rabbit's MO was *Stop, Look, Listen, Act.* She realized that no matter the situation, there is always a choice. The choices are not always pleasant—like burrowing deep underground to escape the firestorm--but they were *her* choices to make.

As a Shaman and a writer, I often see how the techniques of one calling translate into the other. By using Rabbit's *Stop-Look-Listen* when I have a question, I am able to produce stories like this one.

ABOUT THE AUTHOR

Grace Gemini is a Shaman, author, and artist. In her own words:

I am highly focused on the similarities between so-called "ancient Wisdom" and the modern study of Reality Theory. Through comparison and allegory, I try to re-interpret what we call "ancient Wisdom" using terminology appropriate to our day, in order to help modern people understand what was really being said. I have spent over 15 years in the study of Shamanism, but I do not adhere solely to that paradigm. I draw from the teachings of Abraham-Hicks, Bashar/Darryl Anka, Serge Kahili King, Dr. Otha Wingo, Lynne McTaggart, Wayne Dyer, Louise Hay, Ted Williams, Moohji, Buddha, Khalil Gibran, Deepak Chopra, Dr. Paul Pearsall, Bhante Henepola Gunaratana, Paulo Coelho, Shunryu Suzuki, the Bible, the Lotus Sutra, Thomas Moore, St. Augustine, Kenneth Meadows, Viana Stibal, Max Freedom Long, and many, many others.

www.ingramcontent.com/pod-product-compliance
Lightning Source LLC
Chambersburg PA
CBHW040027050426

42453CB00002B/24